MUSICIANS and THEIR INSPIRATIONS

BEYONCÉ and WHITNEY HOUSTON

Voices of a Generation

Tom Jackson

Lerner Publications ◆ Minneapolis

Lerner Publications Company
An imprint of Lerner Publishing Group, Inc.
241 First Avenue North
Minneapolis, MN 55401 USA

For reading levels and more information, look up this title at www.lernerbooks.com.

Main body text set in Eurostile LT Pro.
Typeface provided by Linotype.

Library of Congress Cataloging-in-Publication Data

Names: Jackson, Tom, 1972- author.
Title: Beyoncé and Whitney Houston : voices of a generation / Tom Jackson.
Description: Minneapolis : Lerner Publications, 2024. | Series: Musicians and their inspirations | Includes bibliographical references and index. | Audience: Ages 8-12 | Audience: Grades 4-6 | Summary: "Beyoncé and Whitney Houston have more than just their soulful singing in common. From fame to fortune to charity work, young readers discover how Beyoncé follows in Houston's footsteps"— Provided by publisher.
Identifiers: LCCN 2023048474 (print) | LCCN 2023048475 (ebook) | ISBN 9798765626672 (library binding) | ISBN 9798765629086 (paperback) | ISBN 9798765635643 (epub)
Subjects: LCSH: Beyoncé, 1981---Juvenile literature. | Houston, Whitney—Juvenile literature. | Singers—United States—Biography—Juvenile literature.
Classification: LCC ML3930.K66 J33 2024 (print) | LCC ML3930.K66 (ebook) | DDC 782.42164092/2 [B]—dc23/eng/20231013

LC record available at https://lccn.loc.gov/2023048474
LC ebook record available at https://lccn.loc.gov/2023048475

Manufactured in the United States of America

1 - CG - 7/15/24

TABLE OF CONTENTS

Introduction

Beyoncé (center) got her big break as part of Destiny's Child, along with Kelly Rowlands (left) and Michelle Williams (right).

In May 2003, one of Beyoncé Knowles' biggest dreams came true. She was in Las Vegas, Nevada. Organizers had asked her to perform at the VH1 Diva Duets charity concert. Beyoncé took the stage with Whitney Houston. They sang Stevie Wonder's "Higher Ground" with several other singers. It was a memorable experience for Beyoncé. Houston was one of her greatest inspirations in music. "So many of my life's memories are attached to a Whitney Houston song," Beyoncé said.

The two first met several years earlier when Beyoncé was just fifteen. At that time Beyoncé's group, Destiny's Child, was becoming famous, and Houston was already a fan. The band members met Houston by chance in a hotel. The older singer performed the group's big hit "Say My Name" to them in the lobby.

Beyoncé also sings Houston's songs. "I Will Always Love You" is one of Houston's most famous songs. When on tour, Beyoncé sometimes sings the first verse as an introduction to her own big hit "Halo." Just like Houston, Beyoncé knows that her success comes from working hard to be the best singer she can be.

Whitney Houston was one of the biggest stars of the 1990s.

CHAPTER 1

Young Stars

Both of these musicians began working in the music industry when they were young. Houston was always a solo act. Beyoncé rose to fame as part of a three-member group.

Houston was born in 1963 in Newark, New Jersey. She grew up in a musical home, and her mother, Cissy, was a Grammy-winning singer. She took singing lessons from her. Houston met many world-famous singers under her mother. These included Houston's cousin Dionne Warwick and Aretha Franklin, who became her honorary aunt.

As a child, Houston sung in a church choir. She also learned to play the piano. As a teenager, she began working as a session singer and sung backing vocals on other artist's tracks. In 1981, Houston became a fashion model.

Houston attending a charity gala with her mother in 2010

Whitney Houston performing "I Wanna Dance With Somebody (Who Loves Me)" during a concert in 1991

However, Houston's first love was singing. She recorded demos of famous songs to show to record companies. At just nineteen, Houston signed with Arista Records. Her first album sold twenty-five million copies and had four number-one hits.

Destiny's Child

Beyoncé Knowles was born in 1981 and grew up in Houston, Texas. She began singing and dancing at school. When she was eight, she joined the group Girl Tyme. Girl Tyme performed at talent shows across the United States, including ones shown on television.

Beyoncé's father became the group's full-time manager. He changed the lineup and helped the members audition for record companies. The group eventually signed with a company and changed its name to Destiny's Child.

After several lineup changes, Destiny's Child became a trio in 2000.

COOL CONNECTIONS

Houston was a big fan of Destiny's Child and gave them encouragement. "Y'all stay together, stick together, love each other," she told them. Even though the group later split up, the members have stayed close friends.

Beyoncé (center) performing at an awards show with Destiny's Child in 2005

Beyoncé was the lead singer of Destiny's Child. The group released their first album in 1998. In 2006, Beyoncé went solo and has remained one of the top-selling musicians of all time.

Beyoncé made many solo appearances even when she was a member of Destiny's Child.

Aretha Franklin

Whitney Houston said that her own musical inspiration was Aretha Franklin. Franklin was world-famous singer known as the Queen of Soul. She was also a close friend of Cissy Houston. Cissy would sometimes bring her young daughter to listen to Franklin in the studio. Houston was inspired by what she heard, saying, "When I heard Aretha, I could feel her emotional delivery so clearly. It came from down deep within. That's what I wanted to do."

CHAPTER 2

Working With Others

Beyoncé and Houston are known for their distinctive voices and singing styles. Houston generally chose songs written by other people. Beyoncé is a co-writer on most of her tracks.

Houston rose to fame singing many genres of music, including disco, soul, and R&B. Her singing career began with gospel music. Many of her songs are about the importance of love, religion, and feminism.

Houston didn't always write her own songs, but she added her unique singing style to songs written by others. One way she did this was through melisma. She was famous for it. She might sing a single syllable of a word and add many notes to it.

Houston (top) sang "The Star-Spangled Banner" before the 1991 Super Bowl.

Hitmaker

Beyoncé writes her own songs. In the early days, she would start out by writing lyrics. Then she would find a melody to fit with them. Later, Beyoncé began working with other writers to help create the end product. "It starts with the title or the concept of what I'm trying to say, and then I'll go into the booth and sing my idea," the singer says. "Then we work together to layer on." This means her co-writers might add details to Beyoncé's own vocals, perhaps by adding a beat or backing instruments.

Beyoncé has a wide vocal range. She can sing high and low notes.

COOL CONNECTIONS

Both artists have appeared in movies. Houston starred and sang in the 1992 movie *The Bodyguard.* Beyoncé voiced a character in and wrote the song "Spirit" for the live-action *Lion King* in 2019.

Beautiful Voices

Houston's style of singing influenced many singers, including Beyoncé. "I, like every singer, always wanted to be just like her," Beyoncé said. "Her voice was perfect." Although Houston and Beyoncé approached songwriting differently, they created songs with their own distinctive sounds.

CHAPTER 3

Hit the Stage!

On stage, Houston could often be seen singing alone. Meanwhile, Beyoncé is known for her elaborate performances with complex dance routines.

Since taking off in the music industry as part of Destiny's Child, Beyoncé has been known for her fast-paced dance routines. Dancing remains an important part of her stage shows. She goes on tour with a large team of dancers. The routines often include pop and lock moves.

Beyoncé has said that she becomes a different person on stage. She calls this person Sasha Fierce. The singer says that Sasha is more confident than she is in real life.

Beyonce performing at a concert in Las Vegas during her 2023 Renaissance tour

Beyoncé wears many different costumes during her shows.

Houston sang many slow love songs. She performed them by herself on stage.

Using Her Voice

Houston owned the stage in different ways. For her upbeat songs, she would often have dancers performing around her. Mostly, she let her clear and powerful voice take center stage. She often sang alone.

Houston chose brightly colored and light-fitting outfits that were easy to dance in. She often changed outfits between songs. Later in her career, Houston began wearing glamorous gowns. She also sometimes wore fur and sequins with jeans and a T-shirt.

Houston often wore fancy clothes on and off stage.

Beyoncé performs in a costume created by fashion designer David Koma.

Putting On A Show

Beyoncé's stage clothes are part of every show. During her Renaissance tour in 2023, Beyoncé and her dancers made many quick changes between glittering catsuits and metallic leotards. The costumes were designed by some of the world's most famous fashion brands. These included Gucci, Fendi, and Alexander McQueen. One of the designers, David Koma, said, "For us, the designers, it is not just an amazing exposure but a wonderful cultural moment to be a part of." He added that Beyoncé herself was very involved in all the details of the clothes.

Beyoncé often has a large team of dancers with her on stage.

CHAPTER 4

Record-Breakers

Beyoncé and Houston are both very successful musicians. They have received awards for many of their achievements. Both of them even hold separate records for receiving the most music awards!

Houston had a long and fulfilling career. She left her mark in musical history. In 1994, Houston won eight separate American Music Awards. This is the most any woman has won in a single year. That same year, she won five World Music Awards, breaking the previous world record. Houston also won eight Grammys and sixteen Billboard Music Awards.

Both Houston and Beyoncé have been to dozens of award shows.

Chart Success

But one of Houston's biggest legacies was her hit "I Will Always Love You." In 1992, the powerful ballad went to top of the Billboard 100 chart. It stayed there for fourteen weeks, setting a new record. The song holds the record for the most physical sales. In 2012, Houston passed away, but her music remains popular. She has sold more than two hundred million albums.

Houston wins the Lifetime Achievement Award at the Grammys in 1998.

COOL CONNECTIONS

Charity work is important to both singers. Beyoncé founded BeyGOOD to help people in need get an education and start businesses. Houston formed The Whitney Houston Foundation for Children and organized Christmas parties for families without homes.

Record-Breaker

Beyoncé followed in her musical inspiration's footsteps. Like Houston, Beyoncé smashed records and created new ones. After more than twenty-five years as a professional performer, Beyoncé has won more awards than any other female musician in history. She has won thirty-two Grammys. That is more than any other musician.

Beyoncé tours the world to sing for her many fans.

Beyoncé has sold more the two hundred million records as a solo artist. Her songs "Single Ladies (Put a Ring on It)" and "Halo" are among the most-listened-to singles in history. In 2023, she went on a world tour and saw more than two million fans. Like Houston, Beyoncé is working hard to create music and put on shows that her fans will never forget.

Your Inspiration

Houston was surrounded by music and world-class singers her whole life. This gave her a leg up in achieving her dreams, but her success came from more than that. She worked hard and learned how to sing.

Beyoncé grew up listening to Houston's songs. She was inspired and wanted to be a performer just like her. She trained hard to become a better singer and dancer. It took many years for her to find success. But the effort paid off.

Who inspires you? They don't have to be someone famous. It could be anyone: your best friend, your teacher, your aunt, or a person in your community. Why do they inspire you? What can you learn from them?

IMPORTANT DATES

1983 Whitney Houston signs with Arista Records at nineteen.

1992 Houston's song "I Will Always Love You" stays at the top of the Billboard 100 chart for fourteen weeks.

1994 Houston wins eight awards at the American Music Awards. She also wins five World Music Awards.

1996 Destiny's Child signs with Sony Music.

2003 Beyoncé and Houston appear at the VH1 Diva Duets charity concert in Las Vegas.

2006 Destiny's Child breaks up.

2012 Whitney Houston dies in Los Angeles, California, at the age of 48.

2019 Beyonce appears in Disney's live-action *Lion King*.

2023 Beyoncé has her Renaissance world tour.

GLOSSARY

audition: a short performance to test the talents of a musician, singer, dancer, or actor
ballad: a usually slow song on the subject of love
collaborate: to work with others to produce something
cultural: of or relating to the art, beliefs, and values of a group of people
demo: short for *demonstration*, a recording meant to show off a song to a record producer
duet: a song performed by two singers
feminism: the political, economic, and social equality of all genders and sexes
genre: a style of music
legacy: a long-lasting impact
melisma: using several notes to sing a single syllable
session singer: a singer who is hired to perform during recording sessions
technique: a way of doing something

SOURCE NOTES

4 Jocelyn Vena, "Whitney Houston Remembered By Beyonce" MTV News, February 12, 2012, https://www.mtv.com/news/14m03v/whitney-houston-beyonce.

10 Luchina Fisher, "Find Out What Happened When Destiny's Child Met Whitney Houston," ABC News, November 6, 2014, https://abcnews.go.com/blogs/entertainment/2014/11/find-out-what-happened-when-destinys-child-met-whitney-houston.

11 Mary Shaughnessy, "Whitney Houston Recalled Conversations with Aretha Franklin, Early Modeling Days in 1985: From the Archives," People.com, August 9, 2023, https://people.com/whitney-houston-recalled-conversations-with-aretha-franklin-in-1985-7574353.

14 Amy Wallace, "Miss Millennium: Beyoncé," *GQ Magazine*, January 10, 2013, https://www.gq.com/story/beyonce-cover-story-interview-gq-february-2013.

15 Jocelyn Vena, "Whitney Houston Remembered By Beyonce" MTV News, February 12, 2012, https://www.mtv.com/news/14m03v/whitney-houston-beyonce.

LEARN MORE

Beyoncé: Official Website
https://www.beyonce.com/

Britannica Kids: Beyoncé
https://kids.britannica.com/kids/article/Beyoncé/631685

Britannica Kids: Whitney Houston
https://kids.britannica.com/students/article/Whitney-Houston/311743

Kawa, Katie. *Beyoncé: Making a Difference Through Music*. New York: KidHaven Publishing, 2022.

Nagadya Isdahl, Nansubuga. *Beyoncé*. New York: Abram Books for Young Readers, 2021.

Smith, Elliott. *Black Achievements in Music: Celebrating Louis Armstrong, Beyoncé, and More*. Minneapolis: Lerner Publications, 2024.

Whitney Houston: Official Website
https://www.whitneyhouston.com/

Wilkins, Ebony. *Beyoncé: Queen of the Spotlight*. New York: Random House Children's Books, 2020.

INDEX

PHOTO ACKNOWLEDGMENTS

Image credits: Featureflash Photo Agency/Shutterstock.com, p. 4, p.5; Debby Wong/Shutterstock.com, p. 7a; Stefano Chiacchiarini '74/Shutterstock.com, p. 7b; DefenseImagery/Wikimedia Commons, p. 8; Robert Hoetink/Shutterstock.com, p. 9; Sbukley/Dreamstime.com, p. 10a; Tinseltown/Shutterstock.com, p. 10b; Skyhawk/Shutterstock.com, p. 11a Gyvafoto/Shutterstock.com, p. 11b Stefano Chiacchiarini '74/Shutterstock.com, p. 11c; Lander.pauwels2006/Wikimedia Commons, p. 13a; Gorodenkoff/Shutterstock.com, p. 13b; Everett Collection/Shutterstock.com, p. 14; Kraft74/Shutterstock.com, p. 15; Frank Micelotta/PictureGroup for Parkwood/Shutterstock.com, p. 17a; A.RICARDO/Shutterstock.com, p. 17b; PH2 Mark Kettenhofen/Wikimedia Commons, p. 18; Fabio Diena /Dreamstime.com, p. 19a; s_bukley/Shutterstock.com, p. 19b; Raph_PH/flickr.com, p. 20, p.21, p.26; Featureflash Photo Agency/Dreamstime.com, p. 23a; s_bukley/Shutterstock.com, p. 23b; Featureflash Photo Agency/Shutterstock.com, p. 24. Cover: Raph_PH/flickr.com; s_bukley/Shutterstock.com.